D1234354

I Tola You A Million Times...

Building Self-Esteem in Young Children Through Discipline

by Judy Snyder

Family Connection Publications ● 1989

Library of Congress Catalog Card Number: 88-84049

ISBN: 0-9621931-0-0

Published by:
Family Connection Publications
P.O. Box 406
Cary, Illinois 60013

To my parents, John and June Dixon

Within the fabric of the generations, the important truth is the love we pass from one to the other. And the family is where we learn love, live it, believe it, and God willing we gratefully pass it on.

John G. Dixon

Table of Contents

Introduction

Parenting can be the most challenging, rewarding endeavor a person can undertake. And becoming a parent is, in my opinion, a privilege. A privilege that requires skillful education. But, I didn't always feel this way. I had to be convinced.

Back in 1982, we had one child, Bradley, eighteen months old. An eighteen-month-old is often described as a tiny person moving on a one-way track--a track of his own. Our toddler was no different.

Since I was the youngest in a family of two, I had no idea how to parent and discipline a toddler. My son's favorite word was "no." He seemed to ignore many of my requests, and I soon realized I needed some help.

Prior to my parenting career I had worked as a learning disabilities teacher. I knew I loved kids, and I believed my teaching experience would erase any doubts I had about becoming a good mother.

But the toddler years taught me that having a teaching degree, or loving other peoples children, did not give me the tools I needed. Eventually I realized that being a loving, positive, and effective parent required the parenting skills I had yet to learn and acquire.

Becoming a loving and effective parent clearly takes time, patience, insight, and education. The fact that we were all once children ourselves does not automatically qualify us to be competent parents. Skillful competence takes time. And we need to look at parenting as a long-term commitment that requires love, skill, learning, and practice.

Children have a very real dependence on us as parents. They need our guidance as models. Beginning as an extension of us, children will pick up on our own feelings of self-worth. They soak up what we model--self-confidence or self-condemning--and reflect those feelings themselves.

The year our son turned eighteen months I began teaching the nationally recognized program, "Systematic Training for Effective Parenting." (See resources.) Some parents pick up a craft or hobby to get out of the house, I like to teach. So, just for fun, I began teaching parenting classes with enthusiasm and reservation. What did I, a parent of one toddler, have to offer?

I found I was becoming an effective group leader, and a sensitive listener. I really enjoyed interacting with other parents. The exchange of similar joys and concerns affected me deeply. We had the same problems. We shared the same happy moments. I felt good about my parenting style and the skills I was learning.

When I became pregnant with our second child, Kelly, I began to realize the parent groups had come to mean more to me than an opportunity to get out of the house. They had become a part-time career. A career so enjoyable that it seemed to be no work at all.

In 1984, I started focusing on the discipline needs of young children, and I was trained to lead another nationally recognized program, "Responsive Parenting," by Saf Lerman. Then in 1987, I took a training workshop from Don Dinkmeyer, Ph.D., one of the authors of the "The Effective Parent." This training and the parent groups I lead, led me to write my weekly newspaper column, "The Family Connection," and the compilation of this book.

Becoming an effective and skillful parent requires a conscious choice to develop strong, healthy, family bonds, and thereby foster good self-esteem. For both parents and children. The single most important skill we can teach our children is how to like themselves for simply "who they are."

1
What is Your Parenting Style?
How Do You Discipline?

What is Discipline?

Discipline means: to teach, to explain to, to show children the sense in acting in acceptable ways; to help them develop their own inner feelings of self-control.

Teaching children with discipline that is effective is certainly time-consuming, but well worth the effort. If discipline is handled properly, parents will have children who develop a healthy self-esteem, and who are well-liked by others.

The greatest gift parents can give their children is good feelings about themselves. Healthy feelings of self give children a strong sense that they are loved, "just for who they are." Feelings such as these enable them to enjoy loving relationships with family members, and develop friendships with others.

There are many ways to discipline young

children, but some are more effective than others. The effectiveness oftentimes depends on the quality of the relationship between the parent and child.

A parent who shows respect for her child through word and action, will most likely have more consistent follow through from that child with reminders, warnings, or requests for proper behavior.

To explore further the importance of mutual respect, effective discipline and building self-esteem, let's describe two styles of parental communication: *Traditional and Positive.*

Consider the following examples:

Traditional Style: "Stop running in the house, Bobby. I said, stop running. WHAT ARE YOU, DEAF?!, I'VE TOLD YOU A MILLION TIMES, STOP THAT RUNNING! DO YOU WANT A SPANKING?" (Parent threatens and does not follow through, or follows through with a spanking.)

Positive Style: "Stop running in the house, Bobby. Stop! You have a choice. You may stop running in the house or take a time out now!" (Parent respectfully states expectations to the child and follows through with a time-out.)

These examples clearly depict two styles of parenting. Parents who follow the traditional style learned it from their parents. So one generation replays the same words, tone of voice, and methods to the next generation.

On the other hand, other parents recognize what their parents said to them during childhood, but alter tradition by being loving and firm, and by choosing their words carefully.

The early years are a crucial time for parents to learn or change traditional parental remarks. Children mimic our choice of words and how we say them. They are sensitive to our statements, warnings, requests, choices and limits. They want to please us.

When parents say, "Behave yourself. DON'T YOU KNOW ANY BETTER?" they often don't realize that young children don't understand the request. Children wonder, "What is it that my mom wants me to do?" Young children require expectations that are clearly stated, concise, and immediate.

As a parent educator, I have found that parents want practical guidance for effective communication and discipline that builds self-esteem in children.

What parents say to their children, and how they say it, surely affects their relationships. Parents' words and attitude can promote defiance or cooperation, caring or indifference, love or hate. It is their words, and the attitudes behind them, that make relationships loving and strong, or hurtful and strained.

Children learn from our choice of words and echo them with us, and others. While interacting with family members or friends, they can be heard spouting hurtful comments. "Stop acting like a baby," an older sibling says to his four-year-old sister. "What a brat!" Children, like their parents, follow tradition too.

Even the best of parents find themselves using words that don't build self-esteem. And a healthy self-esteem is built upon recognizing a child's unique strengths and qualities, using constructive criticism, and disciplining effectively. Each of these skills can be learned.

A child's self-concept is easily damaged by hurtful criticism or thoughtless words said in anger. Naturally, we can all fall off the bandwagon at times and say hurtful things, but our goal as parents is to make hurtful comments the exception rather than the rule. No parent is perfect, and we all make mistakes. Our children benefit from seeing and hearing us say, "I'm sorry, I was wrong." They in turn will say those words to others.

When parents catch themselves using traditional comments they need to realize they are simply replaying the old tape recorded messages they heard during their own childhoods. When opportunities to praise, teach, or discipline occur, they automatically play that tape and tradition repeats itself.

Parents who seek to become more positive and conscientious about their parenting skills often find the wealth of information confusing. There are many ideas, techniques, and methods to choose from, but parents often know what works best with their children. Parents can learn how to develop their own style of parenting, while using positive words to discipline and thereby build self-esteem in their young children.

The purpose of this book is to help parents feel confident and decisive, to enjoy day-to-day parenting, and to recognize which style: traditional or positive, they most frequently use. Through this discovery, parents will choose their preferred style of communication. Most importantly, parents will acquire the words, skills, and attitudes to be loving and effective parents.

Practicing these changes will be challenging at first, but immensely satisfying when we hear our children choose their own words carefully with others, and see their self-esteem grow.

2

Positive Ways to Express Anger
Choosing Your Words Carefully

Positive Ways to Express Anger

All parents, however well-meaning, say things in anger which they later wish they hadn't. Even simple feelings of irritation may cause usually patient parents to say sarcastic, hurtful remarks to their children.

Parents think they are teaching children how to behave properly with such corrections. Oftentimes they are simply following tradition.

"Don't you know any better?" a parent says to her child who inadvertently overflows her juice glass. Or a parent who disciplines a child for being "bad or naughty" somehow believes that shaming the child will increase his motivation to do better next time.

Parents of school-aged children and teens

frequently say, "I can never count on you to get things done! What's your problem?" Critical words said in anger do not motivate children to act better. Instead, they invite revenge and erode self-esteem.

When I was angry with my children, I found myself using many of the same critical remarks my parents had said to me. I longed to change these statements, so I began to list the hurtful comments, and then developed positive counterparts. And I asked other parents for some statements their parents had said to them to expand the list.

Much like a tape recorder we remember all too clearly the remarks we heard from our own parents as we were growing up. Then, when our emotional buttons get pushed, we play back those same hurtful words.

70 Ways to Choose Your Words Carefully

Traditional Comments:

1. "I told you a million times..."
2. "FATSO, STUPID, DUMMY."
3. "#*%&&#*##*!"
4. "You're so clumsy!"
5. "You're pathetic. Can't you do anything right?"
6. "You stink."
7. "What did we do to deserve an ungrateful brat like you?"
8. "You're a slob."
9. "You're worthless. You'll never learn!"
10. "There must be something wrong with you."
11. "Can't you do anything right?"
12. "I'll do it myself. You'll just ruin it."

Positive Comments:

1. "The rule is..."
2. "(Child's name.)"
3. "I'm so mad I feel like swearing."
4. "You're growing so fast."
5. "Keep trying. You'll get it."
6. "I'm very angry!"
7. "Sometimes you can be very frustrating."
8. "Rooms are for comfort. I need you to help clean."
9. "We need you. We know you can do it."
10. "I have faith in you."
11. "Try again. You can do it."
12. "Let me show you, then you can try."

13

13. "You never learn."
14. "You're a bad girl/boy."
15. "How stupid can you get?"
16. "You make me sick."
17. "Go wash that filthy face." I don't want to kiss a dirty face."
18. "I'd rather not be seen with you."

19. "You're spoiled rotten."
20. "Don't you get it?"
21. "I could kill you. I could wring your neck."

22. "Go ahead and leave home. Nobody else would want you."
23. "I wish you were never born."
24. "You're more trouble than you are worth."
25. "I hate you."
26. "You'll never amount to anything."
27. "You're a pain in the neck."

13. "You can learn."
14. "I don't like your behavior."
15. "I know you can do it."
16. "I'm furious."
17. "Let's get a cloth to wash your face."
18. "You are important to me even when we don't agree."
19. "We need to make some changes."
20. "Let me explain it to you again."
21. "I am so angry about what you did. I'm going to take a walk."
22. "I love you. Let's talk."
23. "I'm glad you're my child."
24. "You're special to me."
25. "We need a break from each other."
26. "I'm so proud of you."
27. "Sometimes I can feel SO ANGRY when you..."

28. "I don't care what you do!"

29. "No child of mine is going to tell me ____."

30. "Stop acting like a baby." "Act your age. Grow up!"

31. "You've no reason to feel like that. You're just a kid."

32. "Stop being so sensitive."

33. "No, you can't sit on my lap. You're too big."

34. "Wipe that look off your face."

35. "What's your problem?"

36. "Just shut-up."

37. "I hate you!"

38. "Not now. Can't you see I'm busy?"

39. "What were you thinking of when you did that?"

40. "I can't believe you did that."

41. "Because I said so. I've lived longer than you."

42. "No! You don't need a reason."

28. "You matter to me a lot. Let's cool off and talk about it."

29. "You're opinion counts."

30. "I expect you to be able to ____."

31. "Your feelings are important to me."

32. "I'm sorry if I hurt you."

33. "I like being close to you."

34. "We will talk when you're ready to solve this problem."

35. "Can I help you?"

36. "Be quiet."

37. "I hate what you did."

38. "I can in ____ minutes."

39. "What were some other things you could have done?"

40. "You've really hurt me."

41. "Those are our rules. We'll talk later."

42. "I can't allow you to because ____."

15

43. "I was never allowed to do that when I was your age."
44. "You don't know anything!"
45. "It's about time. I thought you'd never be ready."
46. "What will the neighbors think?"
47. "You're usually such a good girl/boy."
48. "I can never count on you to get things done."
49. "Why can't you be good like your brother?"
50. "You could do better if you tried harder."
51. "I'm going to teach you ____ if it takes me all day!"
52. "What's the magic word?"
53. "You look terrible. Your clothes don't match and you shoes are on the wrong feet."
54. "You brat."
55. "You're a naughty boy/girl."
56. "Shame on you."
57. "Move when I call you or you're going to get it!"

43. "That is a privilege you're not ready for because ____."
44. "I respect your opinion."
45. "I'm glad you made an effort to hurry."
46. "This is how I feel."
47. "I'm disappointed that you did ____. Or that you said ____."
48. "We are a team. We need to work together."
49. "You are unique. You are special."
50. "You work very hard."
51. "You're good at your own special skills."
52. "Say please and thank you."
53. "I'm happy you dressed yourself."
54. "You're difficult."
55. "What you did made me feel angry."
56. "I'm disappointed."
57. "It's time to come now."

58. "I'll teach you to hit people." (Parent spanks child.)
59. "How many times do I have to tell you!"
60. "Do you want a spanking?"
61. "Stop or you'll get it."
62. "You're being punished or You're on punishment."
63. "I'll beat your butt if you don't stop ___ now."
64. "Behave yourself."
65. "Stop ___ or I'll smack you."
66. "I'm spanking you because you hit your sister."
67. "Sit in the corner until I tell you to come out."
68. "Say that word one more time and I'll wash your mouth out with soap."
69. "Get out of my way."
70. "I'll make you pay for that."

58. "People are not for hitting. Take a time-out."
59. "You have a choice: You may ___ or ___."
60. "Time-out for ___."
61. "Stop ___ now!"
62. "You need time to stop and calm down."
63. "I need cooperation NOW!"
64. "Couches are not for jumping."
65. "Stop or take a time-out."
66. "Time-out for hitting your sister."
67. "Take a time out until you can join us again."
68. "I will leave the room whenever you speak to me using mean/swear words."
69. "I need some time to myself."
70. "I need some time to feel better about you. Then we can talk and hug."

We parents can choose better ways to express our anger, and positively motivate our children. We simply need to play back the tape from our own childhoods, and substitute positive statements for the traditional ones we may have heard and repeated.

Time and time again, "Choose your words carefully" has brought chuckles and tears to the faces of parents. We can choose to follow tradition, or change. It is possible to change the way we talk, to become more skillful and positive at expressing our emotions. And when we have the courage to make these changes, our children will develop higher self-esteem, worth, dignity, and compassion for others.

What more could we want?

3
Helping Children Develop Mutual Respect
Ten Positive Discipline Methods That Work

Helping Children Develop Mutual Respect

Positive discipline that works, for both parents and children, is dependent on the quality of the relationship that exists between them. Parents with children who enjoy a loving relationship based on mutual respect seem to have an easier time living together and learning from each other, while developing a family atmosphere based on cooperation.

When parent-child relationships are based on mutual love and respect, parents have children who follow rules and limits more easily. And children have parents who communicate and discipline respectfully.

This mutual respect strengthens all relationships in the family providing a forum where all members are equally heard and valued.

When disciplining young children, parents are frequently heard saying the words, "You're being punished." This is a common statement they probably began using from modeling their own parents, or listening to others. What is troublesome about that phrase is not so much the words themselves as the attitude they imply, a condescending attitude that invites retaliation from children instead of cooperation.

Punishments are often not related to the misbehavior, and invite revenge. Children feel put-down. The method of punishment does not acknowledge mutual respect between parent and child.

Using natural or logical consequences for misbehavior encourages mutual respect in families. Logical consequences are directly related to the act, and permit the child to choose better ways of behaving.

Children need opportunities to make poor decisions and learn from them. The method of natural or logical consequences encourages children to make responsible decisions while learning that their actions have logical outcomes.

Consider the following examples:

"Susie, stop calling your brother names, or I'll wash your mouth out with soap!"
"Susie stop calling your brother names, or leave the room until you can talk to him kindly."

"John, I'm tired of asking you to pick up your toys. No TV for a week!"
"John, I feel frustrated when I trip on the toys on the floor. Toys that don't get picked up will be removed for a (specified time--hour, day, etc.)"

"Bobby, I told you not to cross the street. You can forget that new toy you wanted."
"Bobby, I need to know I can trust you not to cross busy streets when I'm not looking. You may not leave the yard today but you can try again tomorrow."

I suggest that parents refrain from using the word "punishment" when teaching children rules and values, and use statements that offer choices using natural or logical consequences. Instead, use the words, "You have a choice. You can either decide to cooperate or ____." Offering the choice allows the child to practice his self-control and take responsibility for his actions.

Some parents may feel that punishments like

standing children in corners, washing mouths out with soap, spankings, or sending children to bed without meals are quite effective. Effective they may be at stopping the behavior, but at the same time they invite revenge. Children will focus more on their anger over the method rather than what they can do to try again and cooperate.

Ten Positive Discipline Methods That Work

The following ten discipline methods will strengthen parent-child relationships, encourage mutual respect, and build children's self-esteem:

1) Learn to identify and acknowledge the feelings of your child. When your child comes to you to express his thoughts, ask yourself what he may be feeling. Is it happiness, anger, sadness, frustration, embarrassment, confusion, etc.? Acknowledge his right to feel the way he does and reflect that feeling back to him. "You seem to be feeling sad." Or, "Could it be that you are embarrassed?" Or, "You seem so happy with yourself."

Statements that reflect the child's feelings help him to get in touch with his emotions, to better understand and express himself.

2) Spend time together. Even 15-30 minutes a

day strengthens parent-child relationships. There are countless opportunities to be together. The time doesn't always have to be a planned activity. Take your child to the store, on an errand, for a car ride, or on a walk. Tell your child these times are meaningful to you.

3) Model healthy ways to express anger through words and actions using "I" messages. "I am so angry the milk got spilled...I get frustrated when I don't get cooperation." Statements that avoid using the word *you*, "You spilled your milk again? You never do what I tell you," often turn the child off before the limit registers. Show your child acceptable ways to release anger like: taking a walk, jumping rope, vacuuming a rug, or hammering on wood.

4) Praise and encourage your child frequently and be specific. Say "I love you" often. Listen closely and attentively. Share your opinions with your child. Focus on your child's specific strengths and comment on them.

5) Teach your child problem-solving skills. Instead of solving her concerns for her ask, "What do you think you could do about ____?" Or, "What do you think you could say to ____?" Help your child resolve issues on her own.

6)   Recognize the importance of physical contact. Supply plenty of hugs, kisses, hair tousling, gentle tickling, lap holding, hand shakes, winks, and waves, or hold him from behind and gently whisper in his ear.

7) Give your child clear rules and expectations for desired behavior. "People are not for hitting." "I expect toys to be put on the shelf." "I need your cooperation to come when I call you."

8)   Take time to teach your child social skills. Help your child see the value of sharing toys with other children. Use role playing or pretend play to teach your child the meaning of words like: gentle, cooperation, appreciation, please and thank you, kindness, compassion.

9) Give your child choices, within limits, instead of threats. When you have given your child a warning, and she doesn't follow through, state your rule and give her a choice: "Food is for eating. You may eat your food or leave the table." "Toys are not for throwing. You may play gently with your toy or pick another one." Be decisive and clear-cut with your expectations. Frequently, young children need warnings and choices given many times before they can easily remember rules and follow through.

10) Use humor or excitement to add some fun to life. Tell jokes, listen to funny cassette tapes, dress up in silly costumes, eat breakfast food for dinner or sandwiches for breakfast. Play some guessing games. Let your child play "Mom" for a day.

4
Building Self-Esteem
Loving Our Children and Ourselves

What is Self-Esteem?

Self-Esteem is a feeling that is portrayed in the way a person acts or feels. Characteristically, self-esteem is best described as having respect for, and belief in oneself.

Self-Esteem and Children

A child can have high or low self-esteem. Parents can observe how a child feels about himself by the way he acts. A child who behaves in positive or motivating ways is reinforced to continue those feelings and actions. This child is pleased with who he is and what he can do.

Some characteristics that are associated with high self-esteem are acting independently, assuming responsibility, feeling lovable and capable, influencing others, tolerating frustration well, and pride in accomplishments.

A child who exhibits a negative or low self-esteem tends to be unhappy with who he is and what he can do. A child with low self-esteem may avoid situations that provoke anxiety, feel that others don't value him, demean his own talents, blame others for his own shortcomings, be easily influenced by others, or defensive, and easily frustrated.

Feelings of self-esteem fluctuate. We cannot expect feelings and behavior to remain constant. We do need to become concerned, when characteristics of low self-esteem are prominent in our children's lives, and take the necessary steps to help change those feelings by observing and commenting on their individual character strengths.

Self-Esteem and Parents

Parents who possess a strong sense of self-esteem have a great advantage in life. A healthy self-esteem carries them through life's difficulties and triumphs.

Having good self-esteem means parents have belief, self-respect and pride in themselves. Positive feelings of self are not dependent on what they own or what kind of home they live in. It makes no difference if the family is headed by one parent or two. Or what kind of car they drive, the vacations they take, or who they rub shoulders with.

A positive self-esteem comes from the strong feelings we have inside, about ourselves. And, since our children look to us as models, we need to continually ask if we project to them an image of self-respect and acceptance or self-doubt and rejection.

Try asking yourself the following questions and list your answers:

Am I happy?
Am I most often negative or positive with myself and others?
Do I accept myself just for who I am?
Do I take good care of my health?
Do I relax and have fun?
Do I have goals and plans?

After you've reflected on these questions ask yourself what actions are necessary based on your answers. The better you feel about yourself, the more patience, love and acceptance you'll have to give to yourself, and your children.

How Can Parents Build Self-Esteem in Young Children?

Feelings of self-esteem begin to develop in infancy. As parents, we are in an excellent position to help our children attain good feelings about themselves. We can accomplish this by accepting each child as an individual, with unique qualities. But most importantly, our acceptance cannot be dependent on what our child does, or what we feel she should attain to please us.

Developing true acceptance of a child can sometimes be very difficult. Some characteristics a child exhibits can literally drive parents up the wall. Like the child who procrastinates when you are in a hurry. Or the shy child, fearful to speak up for herself. The child who tattles continually on others. And what about the irritable, stubborn, or aggressive child?

Character traits, both desirable and undesirable, directly affect how we feel about our children. And parental feelings and attitudes directly affect children's feelings about themselves

Parents can learn to observe, focus, and positively comment on each child's individual personality strengths and characteristics: like his eagerness, helpfulness, or friendliness.

Parents can also make a concerted effort to downplay, and remain unruffled by their child's irritating character traits. In doing so, parents and children alike will enjoy a loving relationship.

Using Specific Praise and Encouragement to Build Self-Esteem

Frequently, the praise and encouragement we give our child is not specific to her personality. We tend to be more global and general. For example, we might say to our young child, "You are such a good boy," or "You are a big help to Mommy," and "I'm so proud of you."

Comments such as these are loving and helpful to build self-esteem, but parents also need to use comments that are specific to a child's unique personality. In order to do this the following character traits may be helpful.

Look over the traits and list those that best depict your child. Tell your child specifically, what you love and appreciate about them using your list.

Be specific: "You are so easygoing. I enjoy your warmth." "You are such a neat person, so excited and loving." Comments like these build good feelings in children about themselves. Children believe what parents tell them, and they will strive to repeat the actions parents praise and encourage.

My child is:

happy	*eager*	*lovable*
contented	*responsible*	*empathetic*
comfortable	*caring*	*loving*
easygoing	*playful*	*humorous*
pleasant	*warm*	*grateful*
confident	*curious*	*excited*
peaceful	*independent*	*thankful*
enthusiastic	*helpful*	*decisive*
cheery	*fascinated*	*quiet*
exuberant	*cooperative*	*interested*
friendly	*compassionate*	*forgiving*
generous	*honest*	*sympathetic*
neat	*organized*	*patient*
punctual	*courteous*	*flexible*

To some degree we can help our children overcome undesirable characteristics like shyness or fearfulness or procrastination. But most likely, we need to accept them for who they are, build upon their personality strengths, and help them to work with their less desirable characteristics. And, it's through that acceptance that they learn to know, love, and accept themselves.

34

5

Using Time-Out Effectively
A Method That Encourages Cooperation

What is Time-Out?

Time-out is a disciplinary method that interrupts inappropriate behavior by removing the child from the "scene of action." By removing the misbehaving child, the parent is being firm but kind while setting limits, and is communicating respect for the child.

Time-out is a calming period which helps children stop the misbehavior and prepare themselves to return to the scene and make choices about future behavior. It also gives parents time to collect themselves and decide what they will say or do, next.

How Does Time-Out Differ From Punishment?

Both the use of the word punishment and its meaning--to cause to undergo pain, loss, or suffering for a crime or wrongdoing--infer an attitude of superiority. "I am angry or disappointed, therefore you are being punished."

Naturally children need to experience consequences which may be unpleasant for acts of misbehavior. However, these consequences need not cause pain or suffering.

Therefore we need to think of a consequence as a natural result for an act of misbehavior, which conveys an attitude of instruction and respect. "I am angry because...The consequence for your behavior/action is..."

Time-out provides a kind, but firm consequence for misbehavior.

How Do I Begin Time-Out?

At around 18 months of age toddlers can be introduced to a modified time-out. For behaviors like hitting and biting, simply remove the child from the scene of action and state your rule: "People are not for biting."

Between the ages of two and one-half, and three and one-half, your child should be able to understand the words: *calm, stop,* and *wait.* During this age span your child can be taught the process of time-out. Clearly explain when and how it will be used. Walk your child through the steps.

Time-Out--The Process

1) Tell your child when time-out will be used. Some parents use time-outs for hitting, biting, fighting, swearing, and general lack of cooperation when rules have been clearly stated.

2) Decide where the time-out area will be. Show your child.

3) Give your child the choice, "When you are able to come back and (cooperate, stop hitting, etc.), you may leave the time-out area."

4) Enforce the time-out. This may mean walking your child to the time-out area and/or gently holding him from behind.

5) Praise or encourage your child immediately after the time-out. "I'm glad you are playing gently with your brother."

Points to Remember:

1) Use a tone of voice that shows respect for the child. Firm, but matter-of-fact. "You have chosen by your behavior to take a time-out," or "Time-out for hitting."

2) Use short periods of time-out. Time-outs can

be as short as 10 seconds, and no longer than a few minutes. Keeping time-outs short and frequent provides opportunities for the child to try again.

3) Let your child decide when he is ready to leave time-out and cooperate. Being able to choose when he is ready to get up and behave appropriately gives your child a deep sense of self-control and independence. He feels your belief and trust that he can learn to control himself.

4) The time-out area should be far enough away to let the child calm/quiet down, but close enough for him to see what he is missing. Use an area that works for your child, and one that would not be associated with unpleasant surroundings, such as facing a wall, or sitting in a cold or dark area. Another room works well for some children, for others the separation may be frightening. Simply being asked to time-out in the same room can be very effective for children.

5) Tell your child she may return to the scene and try again when she has calmed down and finished any crying, whining, or fussing.

6) Redirect the child to an appropriate activity after time-out and comment on appropriate behavior. "I'm glad you have decided to share your puzzle. I'm pleased to see you smile and play."

Some Thoughts on Spanking

Some parents may feel that by not using more forceful methods like spanking, they are giving up their power. They may feel that more forceful methods show children that they are "in control, making a stand, and demanding respect."

Parents do need to make a stand, warrant respect, and respond to misbehavior. However, choosing discipline methods that teach children to develop *internal* control is far more effective in the long run, then choosing methods that require parental *external* control.

Spanking or hitting children provides a poor model for teaching them to solve problems with others. Young children reason, "I get hit when Dad/Mom are mad. So when I get angry at my brother I will hit him too!"

By using time-out parents are choosing to act in a positive way that teaches children self-control, problem solving, and thinking skills.

6
Making Positive Parenting Work For You

Techniques to Follow-Through

It's easy to forget those things we've read or learned. Therefore, the following 4x4 forms are provided for parents to cut out and display, inside kitchen or bathroom cabinets for easy reference and skill follow-through.

What we see we remember.

What is Discipline?

1) Discipline means to teach children acceptable ways of behaving while they develop their own inner self-control.
2) Children will follow-through more frequently with parental requests when they are shown respect.
3) What is your parenting style--Traditional or Positive?
4) Focus on strengths rather than criticism.

Positive Ways to Express Anger

1) Parents can choose to use positive words when they are angry.
2) Much like a tape recorder, parents remember what was said to them during their childhood and repeat the same critical remarks.
3) What do I want my child to remember about her/his childhood?
4) Remember to refer to the 70 Ways to Choose Your Words Carefully.

Ten Positive Discipline Methods That Work

1) Remember to acknowledge feelings.
2) Spend 15 to 30 minutes together a day.
3) Use "I" messages to express your feelings.
4) Say "I love you" often.
5) Teach problem solving skills.
6) Use a lot of physical contact.
7) Clearly state your rules and expectations.
8) Teach social skills.
9) Use choices rather than threats.
10) Enjoy humor and excitement--play together.

Building Self-Esteem

1) Observe your child. The way he acts tells you how he feels about himself, happy or unhappy.
2) Remember that feelings of self-esteem fluctuate.
3) Parents need to meet their own needs for happiness, health, having fun, and making goals and/or plans.
4) Use specific praise and encouragement to build on the strengths of your child.
5) Remember to refer to the Positive Character Traits list.

Using Time-Out Effectively

1) Time-out is a calming discipline method that stops inappropriate behavior.
2) Tell your child when time-out will be used. Use short periods ranging from 10 seconds to a few minutes.
3) Decide where the time-out area will be. Use an area that works well with your child.
4) Enforce the time-out. Tell your child to return when he/she is ready.
5) Praise or encourage your child when he returns and acts appropriately.

Resources

For more information on positive discipline and building self-esteem in young children, the following books may be obtained from the library, bookstore, or publisher:

Responsive Parenting, by Saf Lerman. Order from American Guidance Service, Inc., Publisher's Building, P.O. Box 99, Circle Pines, MN 55014-1796

Systematic Training for Effective Parenting, by Drs. Don Dinkmeyer and Gary McKay, American Guidance Service, Inc., Publisher's Building, P.O. Box 99, Circle Pines, MN 55014-1796.

How to Talk So Kids Will Listen & Listen So Kids Will Talk, by Adele Faber & Elaine Mazlish. Avon Books, 1790 Broadway, New York, NY 10019.

Loving Your Child Is Not Enough-Positive Discipline That Works, by Nancy Samalin with Martha Moraghan Jablow. Published by the Penguin Group, Viking Penguin Inc., 40 West 23rd Street, New York, NY 10010.

How To Raise Children's Self-Esteem, by Harris Clemes, Ph.D. & Reynold Bean, Ed.M. Published by ENRICH, DIV./OHAUS, San Jose, CA 95131.

Without Spanking or Spoiling: A Practical Approach to Toddler and Preschool Guidance, by Elizabeth Crary. Parenting Press, 7750 31st Avenue NE, Seattle, WA 98115.

Your Child's Self-Esteem, by Dorothy Corkille Briggs. Dolphin Books Edition. Originally published by Doubleday & Company, Inc.

A Very Practical Guide To Discipline With Young Children, by Grace Mitchell. Telshare Publishing Co., Inc., P.O. Box 679 Marshfield, MA 02050.

The Gessell Institute's Child Behavior from Birth to Ten, by Frances L. Ilg, M.D., and Louise Bates Ames, Ph.D., Harper and Row, Publishers, Incorporated, 49 East 33rd Street, New York, NY 10016.

Coping with Parenting 24 Hours a Day

WANTED: PARENTS--Full Time

Opportunity for persons seeking a challenging, rewarding position. Must be available to work twenty-four hours a day, seven days a week.

Requirements

- Clearly communicate love, acceptance, and appreciation.
- Set rules, standards and expectations that are fair and reasonable.
- Must be able to respond patiently to repeated interruptions.
- Must be able to positively express anger.
- Learn to criticize constructively.
- Be willing to change attitudes and feelings about young children as they grow.
- Be skilled at using effective discipline methods.
- Able to strike a balance between being overprotective and underprotective.

Salary: Not tangible, Non-negotiable

Benefits: Enjoyment of a family life that provides mutual love and respect between parents and children. The joy of watching children grow. The opportunity to produce loving adults whose attitudes and skills will improve the next generation.

THE PARENTS RESOURCE NETWORK™

Lecture Library

*"parents
and professionals
working together
to strengthen
families"*

Are your kids driving you crazy?

You are not alone!
These 90 minute tapes of the recorded-live Lecture/Discussions are now available to you; to hear on your own time, as often as you prefer; to ponder when the issues become relevant to *your* family circumstances.

"Whoever said
raising children is easy,
was never a parent!
Thanks for the help
Parents Resource Network!"

THE PARENTS RESOURCE NETWORK ™

Box 3054, Skokie, IL 60076
312-675-3555

PARENTING TAPES RELATING TO CHILDREN - INFANTS THROUGH AGE 5

1. Play Pays Off! How Parents Can Help
2. Overprogrammed Children and Parents . . . at What Cost?
3. How to Say "NO" to Your Children without Feeling Guilty
4. How to Cope with a "Nighttime Crybaby" and Prevent Future Behavioral Learning Problems
5. "Mommy, I'm Scared!" Understanding the Fears of Young Children
6. Academically Speaking: Too Much, Too Soon?
7. Quibbling Siblings: Understanding Quarreling and Competition
8. Power Struggles: Who's in Control?
9. An Evening with Dr. Burton L. White: The Educational Development of Infants and Toddlers
10. Parental Expectations: Striving for "The Best"; What Do We Ask of Our Children . . . and Why?
11. Rearing Secure Children: Are You Building Your Children's Self-Esteem?
12. Positive Discipline: Don't Leave Home Without It!
13. Nutritionally Speaking: Feed Your Kids WELL!
14. Beyond Spoiling, Before Spanking: Effective Strategies for Challenging Times
15. Positive Discipline That Works! Alternatives to Punishing, Nagging, Criticizing, Bribing, and Yelling
16. Imagination in Childhood: Use It or Lose It! Parents Can Stimulate a Child's Thinking Process
17. Examining the Roots of Misbehavior: Understanding Anger between Parent and Child
18. How a Healthy Sense of Self Develops: Strengthen Your Child's Self-Esteem
19. An Evening with Judith Snyder: Understanding the Theory of "TIME-OUT"
20. Sleep Problems: A Question & Answer Session with Dr. Marc Weissbluth

(All proceeds from the sales of the PRN Lecture Library tapes go to support the ongoing work of The Parents Resource Network)

ORDER FORM

Make Checks payable to: **The Parents Resource Network,** Box No. 3054, Skokie, IL 60076

Please send me the following:

_____ Complete (20 tapes) Lecture Library w/carrying case(s) plus 20 individual cases . . $145.00
Add $7.00 Shipping & Handling

_____ Single tape(s) . . . . (each) $ 9.95
Circle the number(s) of desired tape(s)
Add $1.50 Shipping & Handling for 1st tape and $0.50 per additional tape

NAME _____

ORGANIZATION _____

ADDRESS_____

CITY, STATE, ZIP _____

PHONE ( )_____

For additional copies of *I Told You a Million Times...Building Self-Esteem In Young Children Through Discipline* send the coupon below to:

Family Connection Publications
P.O. Box 406, Cary, Illinois 60013.

- -

Please send me: ____ copies of *I told You A Million Times...Building Self Esteem In Young Children Through Discipline*

$4.95 each
Add $1.00 for postage. I have enclosed _____
Make check payable to The Family Connection.

Mail to: Family Connection Publications
P.O. Box 406
Cary, Illinois 60013

_____
your name

_____
address

_____
city, state, zip